# DEDICATION

Beloved, I dedicate this book to YOU!

YOU, the overcomer; YOU, the survivor; YOU, the fighter! All you have GROWN through in your life has led you to this moment in time. This books purpose is to encourage you on your quest to be better. The Bible says that "...all things work together for good to them that love God to them who are the called according to His purpose" (Romans 8:28 KJV). If you love God, then this book is for you. This book will show you how all of your tears were not in vain. Know beloved, you are not invisible, nor are you forgotten. God will never leave or lose any of His children for He is so AWESOME to always make ways of escape for them. One way to spiritually exit from the enemy's camp is to use this book, which is sincerely and lovingly dedicated to you. *Resist Every Demon AND He Will Flee* was written with you in mind. Remember to first submit yourself to the Lord, then, resist the devil AND WATCH HIM FLEE!

-Apostle J

# TABLE OF CONTENTS

# OPENING THOUGHTS

Singing...

Satan, we're gonna tear your kingdom down
Satan, we're gonna tear your kingdom down.
You've been building your kingdom, all over this land
Satan we're gonna tear your kingdom down.
Satan, preachers gonna preach your kingdom down
Satan, preachers gonna preach your kingdom down.
You've been building your kingdom, all over this land
Satan, preachers gonna preach your kingdom down.
Satan, mothers gonna pray your kingdom down
Satan, mothers gonna pray your kingdom down.
You've been building your kingdom, all over this land
Satan, mothers gonna pray your kingdom down.

If you need to keep singing this for a couple of moments, go right ahead, because I need to do so, too. We often need to be reminded of the damage we can do to the enemy's camp. He walks around as a roaring lion seeking whom he can devour. The enemy is always on the prowl. He desires to steal, kill, and destroy. It is never his intention just to see you down and out... nah, nah baby! He desires to make certain you never return to God's good grace again. Are you not tired of the enemy and his coworkers messing with your mind, body, and spirit? Are you not tired of feeling like you are the black sheep in every setting and not just in your own family? Are you frustrated enough with the stagnancy in your life? Are you not ready for your children to act better? Wouldn't you like for you and your spouse to get along in all areas of marriage, not just during sex? Are you ready to put the enemy to flight once and for all? This book will help you do just that. There is a lot for us to come to terms with in our lives and prayerfully this book will give you the courage to do so. Finally, live out what you are saying....come on sing again with me...Satan, we're gonna tear your kingdom down. You've been building your kingdom all over this land Satan were gonna tear your kingdom down.

The Bible says that one can put a thousand [demons] to flight, but beloved God's word also told me that two can put ten thousand [demons] to flight. I don't know about you, but I'm ready to put the demons that believe they have been given rule over me and my life to flight. If you touch and agree with me, we will certainly put all of those jokers and their cousins on the run. Loosen up beloved, so we can get some much needed deliverance together. In Jesus' precious name, AMEN!

Another songwriter sang it best:

WE GONNA CAST THE DEVIL OUT!
WE GONNA CAST THE DEVIL OUT!
OOPS, UPSIDE YOUR HEAD DEVIL
OOPS, UPSIDE YOUR HEAD
WE GONNA CAST THE DEVIL OUT
Let's mean it for real (Keep singing):
WE GONNA CAST THE DEVIL OUT!
WE GONNA CAST THE DEVIL OUT!
OOPS, UPSIDE YOUR HEAD DEVIL
OOPS, UPSIDE YOUR HEAD
Now rock with it:
OOPS, UPSIDE YOUR HEAD DEVIL
OOPS, UPSIDE YOUR HEAD

Beloved, get your war clothes on. This book was not written with the intention to make you feel all warm and fuzzy inside. You will quickly learn that we are going into battle to go get all of the things that have been stolen from us knowingly and unknowingly. God's word tells us not to despise a thief for if he be found, we can make him give us our stuff back seven times over. I declare that the real thief in our lives is found and is being divinely ordered to give you and I all of our stuff back, unharmed, untainted, not bruised nor broken. In fact, I declare that what we get back is in seven times better condition than when we last had it. Like our love, peace, forgiveness, joy, et cetera. In Jesus' name, AMEN!

First things first, you are going to want to grab a journal. If you do not have a journal, you can use a regular notebook. This book is for your eyes only. It will be used to help you communicate with God as well as help you to become a better citizen in His kingdom. Personally, I love to write in my journal, it is a great release for me. I am very confident that once you start to journal you will find it just as rewarding.

I love music, all kinds. The Holy Spirit allows certain musical lyrics, not all, to minister to me in order to help me understand which direction I should be going, what I should or should not be involved in et cetera. For instance, the Lord ministered to me using the theme song from the movie Mahogany, "DO YOU KNOW WHERE YOU'RE GOING TO? DO YOU LIKE THE THINGS LIFE IS SHOWING YOU?" The Lord can use anything He chooses to get His point across to you. So, you may notice that the chapter titles and other references throughout the book contain an occasional secular musical reference. Please note that I am not saying that all music is great for you to listen to as a believer.

However, please just remember to use discernment when listening to any music. Prayerfully, my liberty/freedom in the area of music will not be a stumbling block to your freedom.

# CHAPTER ONE

# SIGNED, SEALED, AND READY TO BE DELIVERED - SUBMITTING OURSELVES

The great songwriter, Stevie Wonder wrote, "OOO baby, here I am signed, sealed, delivered, I'm yours." Beloved, we now have a remix to this song. Sing with me, "YES LORD, HERE I AM SIGNED, SEALED, AND READY TO BE DELIVERED, I'M YOURS." There is a process to obtaining our freedom. There is some work that must first be done in order for us as people of God to walk in true victory.

In the book of James chapter 4 (I personally like the Message version best), which is a great place for us to begin our transformation process in hopes of never returning to that which has held us bound. We must come to terms with what has led us here, how we ended up needing to be delivered, also from whom and from what do we need to be delivered. We can usually see a person in their current state of rebellion, hurt, pain, and anguish and say that you see this current road for them a far off. Then, it is very easy to shake your head and say tisk, tisk. It was obvious that this was going to be their life based on the way they were living and treating others. News flash, in spite of what we may think people are not born evil, mean, and nasty. People do not come out of the womb knowing how to commit crime and how to inflict punishment on themselves and others. This is a learned behavior. There is something that was either taught or caught that caused this individual to behave in this manner. We must always deal with the root of why we do what we do; why we speak the way we speak; and why we behave the way we behave. If not, there is a possibility that we will become ticking time bombs just waiting to explode. We will learn how to control what is inside of us, but we have never actually gotten rid of what is potentially harmful to ourselves or others. All that will be needed is a trigger to set us off. A trigger is anything from our past that has the fragrance of hurt, pain, disappointment, fear, et cetera. Any one of those triggers could be used to send us back spiritually, emotionally, financially, mentally, and/or physically in our current lives.

Stop right now for a few moments to examine your life. Please examine your life but do not judge it. Think about what is going great then examine what is not so great. Now, write it down in your journal. Please write down what is great and what is not so great about your life. Please be honest with yourself. For some of us, it will be the very first time trying our hand at honesty. This is a judgment free book. After all, besides the Lord and me, who knows you are even reading it? Once you have logged the above information, please date it. I want you to notate the dates when the Lord starts to change the not so great things in your life into the great. This will allow you to see how the Lord is actually answering your prayers. This will also build your faith in Him and in His word. Hebrews 13:5 states that the Lord "will never leave thee, nor forsake thee." Throughout the book, I would like to give you examples of what I am speaking. Some of us have only had ungodly and/or horrible examples of how to do things, which is the only way we know how to operate. My prayer and goal is to walk you through this process of submitting yourself to the Lord and resisting the demons in your life so they can definitively flee once and for all.

Your journal entry could look something like this:

Date: 04/21/2013
*God,*
*I was instructed while reading this book called R.E.D. to start this journal. I am supposed to use it to start having open and honest communication with you and for once myself. I was instructed to be as honest as possible with myself. I know I don't have to share this journal with the public at all. I was told that I will eventually find it rewarding. I really hope that comes true since I have not had many rewards in my life that I can say were or are worth mentioning at this time. I was asked to write down things that are going great in my life as well as the things that are not going so great. Here it goes...*
*What is going GREAT?*
*I woke up today; I had something to eat; I haven't cussed anyone out yet, I am going to work*
*What is not going so great?*
*My bills are killing me, my kids are on my last and final nerve, my spouse and I are not acting like we are even married, I don't have anyone to love me, in fact I don't even like myself, I hate my job, I don't even know what I should be doing with my life right now, I am depressed a lot, I don't get along with my parents, not sure if I*

*am going to get kicked out of my house because I don't have money to pay the rent, I got into another fight with that coworker who I can't stand…and so on and so on.*

Did you notice anything about this particular journal entry? There were only a few things positive but an overload of what is not right. Beloved, it is more than okay if your list looks something like this. Honestly, it is because we all need a starting point. Before we can get the help needed for our lives we really have to be honest as to what is just not making sense in it.

We must finally admit what is the root cause of our pain, angst, hurt, shame, guilt, and embarrassment. Whether it was and is due to another person or it was entirely our own fault, it still must be identified. This is a must if you desire for true healing and freedom to take place in your life. Some of us as a result of finally being honest in our examinations may find some water dripping from your eyes. I know you may not be used to what is called crying, however, I reassure you it will be good for your soul. If you are shedding a tear or two or you are finding that you are beginning to feel humble then the process of making the enemy flee from your life is beginning.

One of the most challenging things we can face in the process of gaining healing in our lives as Christians is getting to a point where you are able to stand naked in front of God. Beloved, that's exactly what this first journal entry should bring in your life. If you are truly being honest with yourself right now open your mouth and tell God, "HERE I AM SIGNED, SEALED, AND READY TO BE DELIVERED LORD!"

The word of God says, "Let every man examine himself" (1Corinthians 11:28). Do you know beloved that we are to do that regularly? When I say examine, I mean we should take a thorough look at who we are, what we do, who is in our lives and why, what motivates us, is God REALLY first in our lives. Does our life reflect what we say to people? Examinations should provoke changes and upgrades to our behaviors, mindsets, speech, and even our finances. This should cause for us to quickly see where we are hurting ourselves or others, where we are being wasteful in our time, finances, and health. We will see and own up to our short comings and would want to do something about it quickly. This scripture about examining ourselves is usually in reference to Holy Communion. It also lets us know what we are advised to do before taking part in Holy Communion. If we don't follow what God is saying, then we are taking damnation into our souls. The word also says that taking Holy Communion unworthily is why some have died prematurely. How many times have we taken Holy Communion without examination and repentance? Through His word and now knowing that God desires us to take regular looks into who we are will you continue to take communion without doing so now? Why must we exam ourselves? Well, besides the fact the Bible speaks on it, we must be different than the world. The Lord has a more excellent way for us to do things. If the world's system on morals and character was great, then the Lord would have not mentioned for us to take a closer look into who we are.

What would happen if we choose not to? Honestly I don't know but what I do know is I choose to have a healthy dose of fearing God. I have been out of His will and ark of safety and it doesn't feel well. All this sister knows is that I believe God's word to be true. He is not a man that He should lie, nor the son of man in which He should repent (Numbers 23:19). Are you ready to make your calling and election sure with the one and true living Savior Jesus Christ? Think about it in the natural. We should be going to doctors for regular exams and check-ups correct? Well, in those times the doctor tells you what you are doing right and what you are not doing right. The doctor will let you know if you are in danger of becoming ill or diseased. If that is the case, then they will prescribe a regiment to help get you back on a healthy track. If you choose to follow the doctor's instructions you will become healed. Usually by the end of the exam after your prescriptions have been written, the doctor will let you know when they would like to see you again for what? Another check-up! If we can do this in the natural, then, we most certainly can do it for the sake of our spiritual health. If you are unable to do self-exams, go see a professional. Who is the professional? The professional is your spiritual leader, adviser, counselor, apostle, or pastor. If you do not have one please feel free to contact me. Listen beloved, do not go to the leadership in your life only desiring to hear the great things. Get what you need to get better. Prayerfully, your spiritual counselor will not only speak to you truthfully, but will make sure they are leading you back to Christ. The Bible declares that there is safety in the multitude of counsel (Proverbs 11:14; Proverbs 24:6). Trust His word to set you free today.

What is deliverance? Deliverance is your new found FREEDOM! Beloved, I want to speak a BREAKTHROUGH ANOINTING TO BE UPON YOU RIGHT NOW! A breakthrough is a sudden burst of knowledge from your current lines of resistance. I declare that you will not faint through the days of adversity. I speak that you will have enough strength to bulldoze your way to the places called HAPPY, JOY, LOVE, and KINDNESS. IN JESUS' NAME. AMEN! How do you get delivered? Who or what are you being delivered from? In the context of this book, prayerfully, you will gain deliverance from reading, praying, and journaling. You WILL be delivered from the hands and tactics of the enemy of God. You will be loosed from the chains and fetters that have kept your mind, emotions, finances, and physical body entrapped and enslaved for far too long. The things that have kept you stagnated and trapped have had authority in your life for so long those demonic spirits really believe they own you. NOT ANY MORE!!!!! I DECLARE AND DECREE YOUR FREEDOM TODAY FROM ALL CHAINS AND SHACKLES IN JESUS NAME! I SMASH AND DEMOLISH EVERY UNTRUTH IN YOUR LIFE AND SPEAK WHOLENESS IN YOUR MIND, BODY, AND SPIRIT IN JESUS' NAME ... AMEN

# CHAPTER TWO

# THE ART OF DEFENSE - LEARNING HOW TO RESIST THE DEVIL

Listen beloved, once you have gained your freedom from the hands of the enemy, it is your responsibility to secure your freedom. The enemy was only content when you were with him and his cohorts. Now, that the divorce between the two of you has taken place he is not a happy camper. The enemy is not okay with you being free and walking in your deliverance. In order to know how to resist you must first know and understand what the word "Resist" means. Let's take a look:

re • sist: to exert oneself so as to counteract or defeat

Example: I know I shouldn't have any more cake, but I can't resist.

In the above sentence the word resist means not being able to fight against the temptation of the cake.

When resisting the enemy, you cannot be in agreement with him, his imps, plans, or strategies for you and your life. You must finally get to a place and space where what he is feeding you is unacceptable. In order to go and grow into what the Lord has for you, you must absolutely fall out of agreement with the plots and plans the enemy has set against you. Don't beat yourself up. Because you are now wondering how you ever fell into agreement with the enemy especially when you know that there is no good in him. The enemy is not dressed in a red suit with horns and a pitch fork in his hand. Your real enemy, that which is demonic by nature, doesn't even have skin! The enemy is subtle and cunning. He desires to slither up next to you and to whisper sweet nothings into your ear. One thing you can be certain of is it is whatever it is he wants you to know is that it really is a NO THING.

The enemy for the most part is not trying to scare you to death just to get you to be a part of his organization. He will do his homework to see what it is that tickles you most. What is it the enemy could use in your life that will bring him glory? The enemy would like to control you through your emotions. Your emotions can change as frequently as the weather. Don't be emotionally led, be spirit driven. If the enemy pitches his case or product in front of you on a day where your emotions are not too stable he will win. Instead of resisting the devil so he can flee, you are in agreement with him so he can win. Let's make sure your every decision and action pleases your Father in heaven instead of glorifying the father of lights. The enemy will feed you the negative about everything in your past and present in hopes of discouraging you from entering into the future your Father in heaven desires for you.

The more the devil feeds you, the more it enters your spirit and eventually you will come into agreement with whatever it is he has shown to you or convinced you to believe. We have heard it said that you are what you eat? I say that whoever you have given the greater power to in your life is now your boss. We pride ourselves in not allowing someone to make us their slave, or how no one will ever tell us what to do in life because we say "I'm Grown". Beloved, someone is always in control of you and your decision. It is either the Lord or the devil. There are no gray areas either. The Bible says that greater is he who is in YOU than he who is in the world (1 John 4:4). Who is the greater one in your life? If it's the enemy of God than you are not resisting him you are giving him full reign in your decisions and choices. With that being said, you are not in a place of peace. That is the reason for the restless nights and painful mornings. When the greater one on the inside of you is our Lord and Savior Jesus Christ, the enemy's fiery darts that arise are easily deflected. You will be more than capable of resisting temptations and all thing of that nature.

Resisting the wiles of the devil can be a challenge at times, but it is most needful for your spiritual growth. The enemy wants you to process information and situations through his network instead of receiving and responding in a godly way. The word of God to says that we are to operate in a more excellent way. This way will never give the enemy happiness. When the enemy is speaking death, confusion, and chaos to you, you must resist him. When he is bringing the latest crisis to you about your family and presents it like you are the only one on earth that can take care of it, you must resist. When the enemy has a hold of your heart and refuses to let you forgive others, you must resist.

Resisting comes in many forms, to fight, to defy, to oppose, to repel and my favorite is to with stand. When the enemy is throwing everything plus the kitchen sink your way... all in one hour, you may feel like giving up. But, do you know one of the greatest weapons as a believer is the power to withstand him? How many fights are won with people on their backs while lying on the floor? Resist is a Middle English word from Anglo-French from re-sistere means to take a stand. Some of us have never had to take a stand against the enemy. Yes, we have stood up against people and different causes that would only benefit us in the long run. I encourage you to take a stand against the devil, his plots, and plans against you. No fight can be won with you lying on your back on the floor, crying in defeat, nor while being mad at those who are standing around as spectators instead of helping you. You have the power and have been given the permission to stand in the midst of adversity. Some of us have never been shown how to properly fight. Know this that the weapons of your warfare are not carnal but mighty through God to the pulling down of strongholds (2 Corinthians 10:3, 5). The Lord will teach you how to fight, defy, and repel the attacks of the enemy while standing strong and tall through it. Even if you fall while resisting the tricks of the enemy quickly get up, don't stay there, and don't let the spirit of defeat pin you to the floor hopelessness. You can do it! YOU CAN RESIST THE DEVIL AND HE WILL FLEE! Stop listening to the piercing threats of doubt and fear that are ringing in your ears. Start by listening and applying the instructions of our heavenly Father. His word reminds us that we are to follow His voice and not that of another person. Once you have successfully resisted the devil, I promise you he will flee.

Flee: to run away from a situation; to take flight. Do you know that your stand in the things of God will put the enemy on the run? You have the power to make the enemy run from you instead of you running from him. We can so easily take off from the enemy when he huffs and puffs on our doors of life. This simply happens when we don't know the power and authority in which we operate. When something takes flight that means it is full of fear. Listen, you have ran far too long in your life from everything has said boo or gone bump in the night. The time has come for you to stand and to stop fearing the terror by night and the flying arrows by day (Psalm 91:5). Our father has NEVER given you the spirit of fear. He has graced you with love, power and a sound mind (2 Timothy 1:7). Now here are your two options on how to face the fears in your life: (a) You could face everything and run or (b) You could face everything and rise!

Selah

# CHAPTER THREE

# THE KINGDOM OF GOD IS SUFFERING VIOLENCE -THE NEED FOR WARFARE

When you put the enemy to flight in your life and/or in another's life, never think that that is simply it for him:
Matthew 12:43-44 (MSG) states "When a defiling evil spirit is expelled from someone, it drifts along through the desert looking for an oasis, some unsuspecting soul it can bedevil. When it doesn't find anyone, it says, 'I'll go back to my old haunt.' On return it finds the person spotlessly clean, but vacant. It then runs out and rounds up seven other spirits more evil than itself and they all move in, whooping it up. That person ends up far worse off than if he'd never gotten cleaned up in the first place."

Beloved, your freedom from demonic oppression is vital to a healthy spiritual life. This is why you had to go and grow through a lot to acquire your spiritual and for some, physical release from demonic bondages. The enemy would like for you to return to those dreadful places in your life. When you get there he wants your condition to be at least seven times worse than when you last left it. Yes, there is a need for warfare! Stop walking around oblivious to what is taking place in the spiritual realm for your sake and that of others in your care. The enemy will be given a reason to thrive in you. Because your spiritual head is stuck in the clouds, you can see or refuse to face the hard cold reality that people are in need of spiritual freedom...just like what you were blessed to receive. We can be extremely selfish as believers. Once we obtain a certain level of peace, freedom, and happiness in God, we refuse or choose to ignore the needs of others, who are now standing in the dry dark places we once called home.

Warfare: engagement in or the activities involved in war or conflict. Warfare is mentioned by name in the Message version Bible twice. The one of note and that suits our illustration is Proverbs 24:5 (MSG) which says, "It's better to be wise than strong; intelligence outranks muscle any day. Strategic planning is the key to warfare; to win, you need a lot of good counsel."

That's right when you are ready to be freed, there should be a strategy in place not only to arrange your freedom, but maintain it. As the aforementioned verse states, you need a lot of good counsel. Once you have resisted the devil and have him on the run, your next step should be to obtain sound godly counsel that will help to ensure your safe future. The Bible says in Proverbs 11:14 that "...there is safety in the multitude of counselors." Your safety and ability to stay saved is of the utmost importance to the Lord. Again I say there is a need to wage war against the enemies of God; not just a single fight so you can see another day fight again, but war. When war is declared between two parties it is an organized and prolonged conflict filled with strategies, violence, and disruption. Know that your technique, the manner in which you carry out your assaults is what is known as warfare. When you were younger and got into a fight you just did what was necessary to survive. After the fight, you may or may not become friends with the one whom you fought.

However, when war is declared, you will never become friends with your enemy...you, nor your children, or your children's children. There will be a deep seated, mutual hatred between you and your sworn enemy. Best illustration of this is the infamous rivalry between the families of the Hatfield's and the McCoy's, enough said! Now, that is true in the physical and so it is in the spirit.

When you are ready to wage war against the devil, you cannot do so from his bedroom, lying in his bed, beside him! When it is time to be used by God he does not want to find you cooking a scrumptious meal for the enemy and his family. It must be clear at all times whose side you are on and whom you are serving. What do I mean? You cannot be one way in God today and be another way when you think that the eyes of the Lord are not watching. I assure you that the eyes of our Father are in every corner. It is clear that you are not sure whose side you are on; if you think you can fool God. Beloved, you must make your calling an election sure as to whom you will serve ((2 Peter 1:10). The word says that we can't serve two master for either we will love the one and hate the other (Matthew 6:24). What you were freed from should now be a stench in your nostrils. The genuine nasty smell of your past failures, faults, traps, and shame should lead you to a specific passion for search and rescue missions for the Lord. Your battle scars and old wounds should now cause for you to seek out those who are in need of the same freedom you were awarded. Your new found passion for freedom in God will cause your spirit to rejoice in your newly obtained liberty. The Bible says for where the spirit of the Lord is there is liberty (2 Corinthians 3:17). There are some people who desire to be freed, healed, and delivered, but lack enough strength or will power to go get what is needed for their lives. This is why it is so very important not to forget where you came from or what you were delivered from. When you truly yearned to be free, the Lord sent just the right combination of anointed individuals that were able to bring the true light of God to your situation. Prayerfully, this book will encourage you to go after those who are lost and in need of the true and living Savior.

# CHAPTER FOUR

# THE THIEF IS FOUND! – ROAD TO FLEEING

Proverbs 6:30-31 says, "Men do not despise a thief, if he steal to satisfy his soul when he is hungry; But if he be found, he shall restore sevenfold; he shall give all the substance of his house." Whew!!! Let us Selah or pause right here for a minute or two. Some may read this and say I don't see a reason to stop and pause at this scripture. Guess what? I'm not even mad at you. Prayerfully, you will feel the need to reflect on this verse and its core meaning in your life once this chapter is concluded. Let's grow through this together.

When I read the Bible especially the King James version, I find that I often times will use a dictionary, Internet search engines, et cetera to get to the real meaning of a word. I really don't want to lean to my own understanding when it comes to understanding what my Father in heaven allowed to be written what I feel is just for me. I would like to break down what I feel are a few key words in understanding this text. Hint: this type of research is the reason for my Selah in the above paragraph. Listed below, here are some of the words in which I needed a little more clarity:

Despise: A strong hate

Thief: One who takes without permission

Satisfy: To meet an expectation

Soul: The core of a person

Hungry: Strong craving; every desirous

Found: To locate; to put a finger on

Restore: To bring back to its original existence

Sevenfold: To have seven times greater

Substance: Material possessions; that which is important

House: A place of living

Here is what I heard in the spirit as I started to work on this chapter. "My people are so overwhelmingly concerned about the likes and dislikes of man. My people have put so much stock into what the world thinks with no regards to My likes, dislikes, or power. My people have failed to realize that this world can only give things that are temporal, but I have sent my son Jesus to them, so that they may have life and have it more abundantly." I also heard him say, "the life My people are choosing to live is not one of abundance, but one of mere existence. My people are choosing to drag, walk, or skip through life with beautifully decorated blinders on accepting the enemy's threats, attacks, and his decisions for their lives, as if I have designed for them to live that way. Beloved, I am hearing the Holy Spirit say "this way of life ought not to be so." When we choose to accept this from the enemy, we are living far below a standard that Jesus himself has already set in place. Jesus said that we are to do greater works than what he has done here on earth. What works are you doing for the Lord? Now, what work are you doing that's greater than the work you have already completed for God? We are so consumed with everything that is not like God. However, when the enemy comes in like a flood, then and only then, do we run to God seeking safety and shelter. We run to places like church services, revivals, prayer meetings and any other church ACTIVITIES that we can find, when we are in desperate need of his protection. When the Lord blesses us and keeps us through our storms, we run out of his protective services that once covered us. We get plugged right back into the world's system all over again.

When we find that we are in these types of cycles our spiritual senses are clouded. Spiritually, our vision and hearing gets clogged; it keeps us from discerning what is right and wrong. Jesus said that my sheep know my voice and a stranger's voice they will not follow (John 10:3, 5). The word know in the Greek translates into an intimacy. When you are intimate with God, you will quickly be able to root out the other voices that have need of you in their demonic camps. If there were no other voices trying to whisper sweet nothings in the children of God's ears, why does the word clearly say that a stranger's voice they will not follow? Beloved, please know the voice of God for yourself. Know that this type of cycle of not being able to know or hear clearly from the Lord will cause your judgment and decision making process to be off. This can be a very confusing time in your life. How do you recognize that your vision and hearing is off? That's easy, when you are sold out to God, there is a peace in you that surpasses all understanding (Philippians 4:7). This peace that only He can provide will be enough to sustain you and any situation you may have to endure. This peace that you have obtained will quicken your spirit when you are on the verge of going outside of God's ark of safety. This knowing of God will not let you rest when you are about to step back into the enemy's camp. Do you find it easy to be with God and all that concerns Him one or two days a week or for just a few hours; then, leave and very easily slide back into everything that is not like Him? Beloved, that's a clear indication of why you are not hearing God the way you should. Now these gray areas in your life will cause for you to not spiritually see properly. With that being said, it would be very easy to mistake who your friends and enemies are in your life. Have you confused who was for you and who was against you? Have you felt paranoid not knowing who to trust? Spiritual discernment is the key to this type of knowing. If this type of clouded judgment can be found in the natural, it so can be done in the spirit as well. Our clouded vision, hearing and discernment can cause for us to lose some precious people and things. Not being in proper position in God could be a great price to pay. All because we could not grasp, who was for or against us. There are usually casualties as a result of our poor decision making or ill advisements.

For example, poor relationships with our children due to neglect, abuse, or choosing everything as well as and everyone over them. If we were clear in our hearing, seeing, and discerning we would have made better decisions/choices on their behalf when we had the initial opportunity. Now, we are wondering where we went wrong and then blaming other people or situations for their behaviors. Our children now become the causalities of our poor decision making. Here is another example: we were diagnosed with health issues. Doctors told we must take medicine and change our lifestyle, but we choose not to do so. We live our life to the fullest until we start having our own family. A few years later, our family is now our priority. We really want to see our children grow and are really looking forward to spoiling our grandchildren. However, our health takes a turn for the worst. Due to years of neglect, our health is failing. Our families are now the causalities of our choices to not take care of our health when first instructed. I'm sure you get where

I'm going and the illustrations of what or who the casualties could be in your lives. Well, beloved, I would like to give you a ray of hope. The Bible says that we must be ready to always give an account for the hope that lays in us (1 Peter3:15). Prayerfully, that is what you will gain after this information on Proverbs 6:30-31:
"Men do not despise a thief, if he steal to satisfy his soul when he is hungry; But if he be found, he shall restore sevenfold; he shall give all the substance of his house."

Beloved, based on the above research this is what we know. The Bible says for us not to hate a person who takes things unlawfully. The reason he takes things that do not legally belong to him is because he has to meet an expectation in the core of who he is due to a very strong craving. Then, we see that it says that if the thief is found he has to bring back to everything that was taken unlawfully to its original state. In fact, he has to make sure it is seven times better than when he first took it. Lastly, the Bible says that he will have to give all his material possessions or rather all that is important where he lives over to us.

Selah

Now consider this... All of this time we have spent being mad at a physical person. Do you know your true enemy does not even have skin? Yes, your true enemy is a demonic spirit, messenger of Satan sent to keep you handicapped. You have been handicapped for a great deal of your life. Some of us have been more disabled than some folks who have to live in wheel chairs. Some of us have become okay with the blame game. It is everyone else's fault, but our own. When will we own up to our own wrong doings? Our own decisions and choices have caused for us to lose our joy, peace, happiness, ability to smile, and breathe again? When will we face some hard truths about who we are, and how we got to this current place in our lives? When will we confront the issues that have been plaguing our minds and hearts for far too long? The things from our past that are still going bump, in the night because the hidden things in the closets of our lives are now pushing to be exposed?

If this is you, know that the cry of any demon is LEAVE ME ALONE!!! If you are thinking about yourself and are hearing or thinking you are ready to put this book down, the enemy in your life is ready to be exposed. If you are now experiencing confusion, doubt, shame, guilt, or embarrassment; the enemy in your life is ready to be exposed. Don't stop reading, keep pushing. The demonic spirits that may be manifesting right now, hate light. Not the natural light that we can see, but the light of the Holy Spirit that is shining down upon you right now. See, the spirits that desire to hide deep down inside of you are now being commanded to manifest and to go RIGHT NOW in the name of Jesus. So, the word tells us based on what we have read, for us not to hate the one who is taking things from us unlawfully. Why can't we hate the one who has made it their job to steal our finances, families, possessions, health, spouses, children, peace of mind, and freedom? Remember, the word of God says that all things work together for the good to them who love God and who are the called according to His purpose (Romans 8:28). If the enemy's attacks on your life lead you and your family back to God did it not work out for your good? Know that the spirits that are taking things from you illegally are doing so right in front of you; not behind your back. While you are drinking, drugging, sexing, neglecting, partying, lying, and stealing yourself the enemy is kindly taking everything from you that you will eventually want to hold near and dear to your heart. While you are plotting and planning your next move, or singing your favorite demonic tunes with your spiritual headphones on, the night the enemy came through the front door. He took your keys off of the table of life in front of you and drove off into the thick of the night to go pick up everything that you cursed out or tried to block out in your life. The Bible says that the enemy is doing these things because (1) we have given permission; and (2) the enemy has an expected need to meet at the core of who he is.

Demonic spirits have a very strong craving for everything that the Lord had designed to be a blessing to you. The enemy is not holding a gun to your head; taking greatness and destiny from you. We are handing it over to him through idol and cultural worship of false and other gods. We live recklessly as if the true and living God is not real. God is so amazing as to give us a way of escape. He knows for a fact we are in over our heads. In His word it says, "...But if he is found..." Beloved, the only way a thief can be found is if you are ready to do something about his reckless handling of your life. The thief has always been there in your life, but you considered him a friend, a close confidant. Now that your back is up against the wall, you are ready to become saved for real. It is time to fall out of agreement with those spirits that have been in operation in your life for far too long. Here is my question to you, IS THE THIEF REALLY FOUND IN YOUR LIFE? Once he is located, uncovered, or exposed the Bible lets us know what to expect next. The Bible says that he will restore seven fold that which he has taken. What is the thief, your enemy restoring? He has to restore any and all of the things that you hold near and dear. He comes to steal your joy, love, happiness, and peace of mind. He is craving to take your marriage and children away. The enemy wants to deplete your finances, self-esteem, and your identity. Your true enemy is the one who desires for you to be stripped of everything that could remind someone that you belong to the true and living Savior Jesus Christ. He wants you naked before him in the spirit; if you allow him to steal your mind; he can even make you do it in the natural. Just keep remembering that the word tells us that he MUST restore seven times all that he has stolen from us. Do you know that the Lord through His word does not just stop and say he must give you back your stuff, but it must be given back seven times greater than when it was first taken? The definition of restore is to be brought back to its original state. Now, add seven times greater to that. Yes, no matter what condition your most prized possessions were in when it was removed from you by the enemy, he MUST bring it all back to you seven times greater than the last time you held it, felt it, smelled it, spent it, kissed it, received it, or even looked upon it! Selah

Now, after what was stolen from you have been now brought back seven times greater, the Bible doesn't stop there. It continues and says that he will give all of the substance of his house. What is that? Not only are you getting all of your things back, but he must also give you in return all that is near and dear to him. He must give you all of his stuff that is in his house that has a place of value. Our Father is about the overflow. You receiving your things back is just not good enough for the God we serve. He desires that we have life and have it more abundantly. Baby, prepare yourself for the overflow from the overflow. This is encouragement for you to go after the thieves in your life. You should be motivated and empowered to receive what is rightfully yours. Our pitfall is that when we see our brothers, sisters, parents, children, and other humans as thieves instead of the true evil spirits in operation. Beloved, again don't hate your family and friends. The real thief has been located and the next season is your life is on its way. It's called DUE season. For everything that is due to you shall arrive very shortly. Yes, together we will make the devil flee!

CHAPTER FIVE

# THERE IS A FLOW - HOW TO GET YOURSELF AND OTHER FREE

Examples of my experiences ministering deliverance
(Names and locations have been changed)

There is absolutely no way the Lord can use you in any area of ministry, but especially in the areas of intercessory prayer, the prophetic, and deliverance, if you don't have a heart for His people. We must always be concerned for another person's salvation even when they are not concerned about it. If your flow in the spirit is in the areas the previously mentioned areas, people going through their deliverance process should never leave embarrassed, full of shame, and with regrets as a result of you. Put yourself in their shoes. How would you feel after getting free in the spirit and/or in the natural and the person whom the Lord used to help unlock the doors of your bondage was now looking at you funny? Perhaps, they are whispering with others about what went on or what was exposed during your deliverance session? Consider how challenging it must be to face the people the Lord used to get you to freedom. Would you not want people to have compassion for you? Would it not be a little easier after receiving deliverance that you had a support team ready to share God's love and kindness with you once your session was done? Listen, the follow up care after someone receives deliverance is just as important as the initial counseling and the actual deliverance sessions. Once a person has received deliverance and the experienced prophetic they are very sensitive in the spirit. Be very careful not to cause the person who received deliverance to regret ever meeting you.

Before you can go into the enemy's camp to get others released, you must first free yourself. In the physical, what kind of freedom can you bring to another person with your own hands and legs bound? Now, in the spirit, what kind of breakthroughs can others gain from you, if you are walking around spiritually shackled in your own mind, heart, finances, tongues, et cetera? The person in need of physical and/or spiritual freedom will look at you as if you are crazy. They will be left more frustrated than anything because you are on the scene in their life, in which is one of their most distressful times, ill-equipped. You are there, but unable to do anything about where they are; you do not possess the keys to unlock them from the reality of the hell that they are living daily. The same passion and desire you have for others to walk in their liberty, you must first want for yourself. Bound and oppressed people will respond to you better when they see and know that you too were once bound, but are now free. They will know that you are free indeed because your walk, talk, and mindset will reflect it. The world can smell a fake and a phony a mile away. They, too, can discern when the truth is not setting them free or when it is not even on the scene. They can also see when your tree which should be an extension of your life is not bearing fruit, or the fruit being produced is rotten, moldy, and disgusting.

Stop using religious jargon, clichés, and rhetoric just to prove you are free from the enemy's camp. Your seasoned tongue that will be full of grace along with your compassionate heart that is clothed in kindness and understanding will be all the individual needing freedom will require and most importantly, see (Colossians 4:6). The enemy can even trick you into believing that it is best to only be concerned for another. Beloved, do not fall for this tactic! If you only are concerned for others and not taking any thought for yourself, you are placing yourself in a position of never examining yourself. If you never stop to examine yourself like the word of God says, then all you are left with is your own understanding. Your own understanding can leave you with blinders on. You can start to honestly believe that there is no reason to repent, because there is no fault in you. You can start to become prideful, because the enemy has told you that you are so great at intercessory prayer, deliverance, and in the prophetic that you do not need to ever do any kind of spiritual checkup.

Warning: DO NOT ALLOW THE ENEMY TO PUFF UP YOUR HEAD!

He will fill you up with hot air while causing another to sharpen the pin they will use to burst your bubble. While you are lying flat on your back due to shame, guilt, and embarrassment; he will be on the sidelines laughing out loud. How do we go about getting the freedom for ourselves we so desperately need in our lives? The Bible says to let every man examine himself (Corinthians 11:28; 2 Corinthians 13:5). To examine means to take a close look. Beloved, I speak this by permission and not by commandment. We need to honestly take a closer look at ourselves, our behaviors, mindsets, and heart motivations; this will aid us in trying to align ourselves with the word of God. After this examination, we would need to yield ourselves immediately to the Lord for His correction and redirection.

There is absolutely no way you can see all of your blemishes, indiscretions, and really believe that our Father in heaven is pleased with your lifestyles and behaviors. Yes, God hates the sin, yet loves the sinner. But guess what? Excuses do not explain nor do explanations excuse. Do not think God does not see the foolishness in our heart and actions. Know that you will never be able to get over on God. He knows when we are attempting to only give him lip service with no real intention of a positive change in our minds or hearts. With that being said, purpose to have genuine, open, and honest communication with the Lord... this is called prayer. Spend a little time with him and watch how much your heavy burden will be lifted.

When you are honest with Him, He will share some truths to you about you. Once this happens, humility will now be allowed into your life. Humility will cause for you to run and make a mends with every person in which you have had an issue. Humility will cause for you to have such gratefulness towards God, who is the one forgiving us of our sins, which are many. Humility is the remedy to soften a hardened heart. It will also cause for your speech to be kinder and gentler. You will know you have experienced deliverance in different areas in your life when you now have a disgust for the very thought of what had you bound. There will be such a horrible distaste for what you have been freed from that it will break your heart to see others dwelling in that place. Since you have come from the same situation, you will be very sensitive to the person and will discern quickly what is needed to lose them from the yoke of bondage.

Deliverance is a process. In order for the enemy not to ensnare you again, you must make sure you are no longer playing in his playground. Once this is clear to you, you will make sure as to convey this to the person who is trying to live a life that is now pleasing unto the Lord. Once the Lord can trust you with people whom are being delivered from your predilections, He can trust you with other people that you are coming out of places that you have never experienced. Hurt is hurt; being away from the Lord is the universal tone no matter the bondage description or the length of time in it. When the anointing of God is upon you to minister deliverance, you will no longer see the person. You will see their need to be free.

## CASE STUDY: SISTER BLESSED, PORTRAIT OF CHILDHOOD HURT

Back Story: Sister Blessed was a prostitute in the late 1980's in Philadelphia. She had a very rough upbringing as a child. To escape her pain she turned to sex for money and using drugs. Sister Blessed was looking for anything that would help her to forget the heavy amount of pain she was in daily. The enemy convinced her that what she needed was to numb the pain, just like the Novocain used in dentist offices. This was her daily goal. What the enemy failed to let her in on was that each day her pain was going to still be there. If it was up to him, he would make sure her level of pain and agony was going to be worse than the day before. While she was trying to find the next thing that would take the pain away she ended up in a very bad situation. One night while prostituting, a male took her back to his home. Sister Blessed thought that she would go in, do what she did best, and leave with a pocket full of money. Instead, that never happened...Sister Blessed ended up in a house of horrors. The man that she went home with that night took her on a fateful trip...into cannibalism. He was into killing prostitutes and eating them. He kept her in his home along with others. This man repeatedly raped and tortured her for over 10 years until he was found out. She was the only one to make it out of that house alive. How did I meet Sister Blessed? I am glad that you asked.

Sister Blessed came for a visit to a church in which I belonged. I had just finished my first 30 day fast. I read in His word that there is a kind of deliverance that will only come by fasting and prayer (Matthew 17:21; Mark 9:29). I promise you I did not go to church looking for these kinds of spirits. There was a call for prayer at the altar. I sat in the very far back of the church with the youth. The youth and I had just returned from a weekend retreat. The prayer at the altar was powerful. It was at least 75 to 80 people standing there hand in hand in prayer. Sister Blessed started to shout Jesus very loudly and very fast. She had on a slinky dress and her breast started to pop out. The men at the men at the altar were now very interested in this young lady rather than the prayer that was taking place. It was amazing to see that the majority of women at the altar stayed focused. They never paid attention to what some of the women and church mothers were attending to and all the while most of the men seemed to instantly get a download that there was a free peep show happening now. The ushers and mothers of the church just kept saying "Praise Him, baby! Yes, the blood of Jesus!"

After a short while, they started to get irritated with her; because now, she was giving their husbands a peep show. I heard the Holy Spirit say to get up and go to this young lady. I prayed as I made my way to her. I could not get to my husband quick enough to alert him that I was on my way to Sister Blessed. Listen; there are not any super hero deliverance workers. You should always work as a team. However, by the time I made my way to Sister Blessed, the women of the church had kindly ushered her right out of the door to a hallway. She was bouncing her way down the aisle like the Disney character, Tigger. They did not know what was wrong with her. They only knew that they had to wrap her up in general and her breasts in particular, and get her away from every husband that stood at the altar. Special note: Prior to this day, I had never seen nor met Sister Blessed. When I met the church mothers in the hallway, they still had no clue as to what to do, nor did they know that this woman was manifesting her demons. I looked around and they kept pleading the blood of Jesus. I got right in the middle of them and spoke sternly. I said, "The blood of Jesus cleanses and protects. This is a demonic manifestation, one in which this church does not recognize." When I spoke this truth, they gave me a look like where did she come from? I looked past all of the flesh that wanted to rise up in the women. I told them that this woman is trying to get out of a demonic situation and every time you plead the blood of Jesus, you are locking those spirits inside of her. Demons cannot cross the blood of Jesus.

By the time I had finished speaking, my husband located me. He later told me that he knew he would find me in the midst of it all. I blessed God that my husband knew the heart of his wife. He knew my heart would not be content just sitting by and watching someone in need of freedom and not doing anything about it. He took the position of praying for me, while I chose to introduce myself to the young lady. Sister Blessed was saying thank you Jesus, but in a demonic voice. The Lord allowed a path to be made so I could get to her. I still could feel the apprehension and jealousy around me. I walked up to Sister Blessed and said "I see exactly who you are and today is your day to leave." While the young lady was bouncing up and down her eyes were rolling in the back of her head. Right after I spoke to her, her eyes returned to normal, and she focused on me. Right after I spoke to her, her eyes came out of her head and focused on my face.

The moment her eyes locked with mine, she released a loud piercing screech. This scared the first responders. I actually did not have any fear; I just got madder at devil. He wanted to embarrass and shame this young lady. He did not want her delivered and set free in her right mind. Instead, he wanted her to stay bound up in his camp. First, he tried to expose her naked body, which was yearning for attention from men during the altar prayer. Then, he wanted her to manifest all kinds of ways that would invoke fear in the women of the church. His goal was to cause this fear to engulf the women of the church so that they would ultimately not embrace her but treat her like a leper. He simply did not care if Sister Blessed came to church; he just did not want her to fit in, get healed, and stay in place of safety. The Lord used me to call out a lot of the spirits in operation that were not easily identifiable. This sister as you could imagine battled heavy low self-esteem issues, self-hatred, and rejection. I learned much later that as a child she was often placed in the corner for disobedience and was left there. During the deliverance process, I saw her in the spirit still in the corner, but as an adult. Her childhood experiences added to her feelings of abandonment and led her to seek attention. However, she wanted more than attention; she wanted to keep that person as a captive audience. Her need to be seen as captivating is how she ended up prostituting. She was able to sell the fantasy that what she was offering and being offered was real love and affection. When I saw the little girl in the corner in a vision she was very immature and naïve. The Holy Spirit quickly let me know to cast this little girl spirit of this adult woman.

As I commanded spirits to leave her body, they responded violently. Again, they wanted to embarrass her any way they could: through either her tears, passing gas, and by urination. Demonic spirits will exit through any opening of the body including your eyes, nose, mouth, ears, genital areas, sweat glands, coughing, and even yelling/screaming. Each time I commanded the spirits to leave they would exit; her body would be dropped to the floor. By this time, those whom I have dubbed the first responders had left me as quickly as they could. You see, when the first demonic spirits responded to my commands, the first responders ran away out of fear and disbelief. I was left with my husband and a nurse. Another preacher came and must have been one of the descendants of the seven sons of Sceva (Acts 19:13-15). When he arrived on the scene, I stepped back to catch my breath. He burst on the scene as a great demon buster and laid a closed bible on her head and started to pray. Sister Blessed turned her head, laid eyes on him, and laughed very demonically. Then, spirits spoke "Oh, we have nothing to worry about he can't move us out." She laid her head back down and possum spirits had her lay there as if she was asleep. I told him to remove the Bible, repent, and do not come back. Right after he left and before I could continue another young man came to watch what was taking place. He pretended like he was there to pray for her. I rebuked him; I told him to follow the other preacher. When true deliverance ministry is taking place, demonic spirits will be commanded to leave the person's body. When this happens they are looking for the next vessel to call home since it was kicked out of its current one (Mark 5; Luke 8).

These spirits would like to be transferred into anyone who is not prayed up or into anyone who is unsuspecting. When true deliverance is being ministered, we must all stay in our lane. Do not get an attitude with those reminding you to be prayed and to stay out of harm's way. When in true deliverance mode a person's life is on the line. This is not the time for petty games or being offended easily. This is a place where some things will be taught but most times is a place where things will be caught. This is a hands on as we grow kind of job. There is no set pattern or formula to use when ministering this way. I had to step up as the leader in the situation. In this particular church setting, men had issues with women leading and being in command. This was not the time to debate that issue. I knew what I knew and knew that these two men were in great danger of demons being transferred to them due to ignorance and disobedience. So for their own good, I strongly advised them to get to stepping.

The God given authority I walk in will not allow me to be pushed or manipulated. This is not me being prideful; rather, I am extremely confident in the One who has graced me with this authority. I fear Him and answer directly to my Father in heaven. I did later try to explain to the men what was going on, but by then their egos were bruised and offense had set in with no room for forgiveness. I was not apologizing for what I did; I just wanted them to understand what was at stake. Remember, I was in an atmosphere where men could not handle a woman being in authority. This young lady had layers of spirits in her and on her. There was no absolute way she was going to get entirely free in one afternoon. However, after about two and one-half hours of ministering deliverance the Lord would allow her to get free enough to breathe and smile again.

Deliverance is a process. The Holy Spirit, the real teacher, the One who will lead you into all truth and righteousness showed up and did what He does best, which is to direct the children of God into a more excellent way to live. I am proud to say this young lady is still living out her deliverance. The challenges of life from time to time still try to get her down, but she manages to hold on. I chose to call her Sister Blessed because at the end of the day, she was really blessed of the Lord. The word says in Isaiah 61:3 that we will receive beauty for ashes, oil of joy for mourning and the garment of praise for the spirit of heaviness. The fact that she was able to come to service bound in religious garment and praise but was able to find freedom through deliverance this Sister IS BLESSED. Her deliverance and maintenance thereof causes me to sing, I'm no longer bound no more chains holding me my soul is resting it's just a blessing, praise the Lord! Hallelujah! I'm FREE!

---

### CASE STUDY: BROTHER LIVING, PORTRAIT OF THE SPIRIT OF SUICIDE:

---

Do you believe in chance encounters? I do not. I believe that nothing happens by happenstance, but instead through the Lord. A few years back I had joined a social media website. I started gaining friends and having a good time. I had accepted a friend request of a gentleman I thought I had gone to high school with. We only said hello to each other and kept it moving. A few months had passed. I received an inbox message asking for prayer. Listen beloved, you don't have to place an advertisement in the church bulletin saying what you do, the Lord will always direct the people who with needs and who need you the most. I read that he was a married man with children and that some things had gone down recently in his life. He felt helpless and was now ready to take his own life. I reread it again. He first said he was only in need of prayer now he is saying he is having thoughts of suicide. When someone reaches out to you for help, we must respond with a yes.

Side bar: Now hear me, your yes does not mean you give everyone money or all that you have until you are left depleted. You know what I mean...giving all your possession and sending your bank account into negative amounts all because you used all of your recourses to help someone get their account out of the negative. This thinking will leave you with an attitude and you will blame God. Saying God told me to help and give everything I have. I promise you missed God on that on. When someone is asking for help we should have a mindset of directing them to best resource in our communities that are designed to help in whatever situation they may be plagued with. The first being our true and living Savior, then to the community at large. Sometimes we have to show them how to go after what is needed to help make their situation better. If we don't have this kind of mindset when asked for help we ourselves will quickly get tired in well doing. We cannot allow leeching and parasitic spirits to latch on and suck the blood from us until we dry up and die. We must be mindful to always direct people back to the Lord for everything. He is our Healer, Provider and Sustainer.

After I read the letter I went into prayer to see if this was something I was being allowed by God to even get involved in. I don't know about you but I am either fully in or fully out of what I commit myself to do. The Holy Spirit quickly told me to have him call me I responded to the message and asked for a call immediately. When he called me you could hear the despair in Brother Living's voice. He immediately started to tell me what was going on in his life. He thought that the best thing he could do for his family and situation was for him to die. He informed me that before I responded to his inbox message, he was sitting in his dining room cleaning his gun so he could kill himself before his family returned home.

He was accused of molesting his wife's 9 year old niece. The niece would spend the night from time to time with Brother and Sister Living and their family. She was never left alone with him. Sister Living even slept with her at night due to girl fun. The niece wanted something from a store and the uncle told her no. The little girl started to get upset with him. She is known to be very spiteful when she got upset. However, Brother and Sister Living had never seen it. She waited a few weeks and told her grandmother (who does not like Brother Living and the entire family knew this) that the uncle had been touching her and made her have oral sex with him. The words from the little girl's lips were fuel for the grandmother. The grandmother sent the cops and Department of Children's Services to his home. Charges were brought up against him. His wife who was there from the store incident to her husband being charged never said one thing to her family concerning her husband's innocence. He told the wife and anyone that would listen that he was innocent. Unfortunately, it was evident that his wife via her actions and language she did not believe him. There was division in the family. Now, the authorities were threatening to take away his three boys out of the home. He thought that if he would just take his own life the family will be repaired and his kids will still be home. He told himself that his family would be better off without him.

We can hear someone wants to take their own lives and shake our self-righteous heads and wave our religious fingers in their face. However, you do not know the agony and turmoil the enemy is placing in front of them. We do not know what demonic sweet nothings the enemy is saying in their ears. We cannot see the shades of hopelessness they are now feeling comfortable in. The Bible say for us not to answer a matter until we hear it in its entirety for it is foolishness and shameful (Proverbs 18:13). Consequently, I made sure I heard his matter out completely and non-judgmentally. When someone feels comfortable to share their heart treasures with you, be appreciative. Respond to them as if it were you who was in need of being talked down from the ledge that you want to be your death spot. The Holy Spirit placed an urgency in my spirit to let me know that he was ready to pull the trigger, while I was on the phone with him. I asked him if he was going to kill himself, then why reach out to me whom he had not spoken to since high school? What was he looking for or in need of? He stated that he told God if He wanted him to live and be here with his family He needed to give him someone who is saved for real and has the power that is needed in his situation. He asked to send that person so he could talk to them NOW and that the person better be able to convince him to not kill himself TODAY and get him free from all of these charges that he was facing. Right after he gave God the demand, he went on to the social media site where we are friends. I am on this social site with my kingdom anointing title in front of my name. He scrolled through the list of names of his friends who were logged on. Out of all of his friends, I was the only Pastor logged on that morning. I responded to his inbox immediately and now I'm on the phone with him understanding the urgency of the situation. I listened to the matter at hand and then asked could I pray for him. I chose not to ask a bunch of questions due to what the Holy Spirit had instructed while listening to him as he spoke. I prayed for repentance, peace, and release of pain. I commanded the spirits of being the scapegoat, blame, guilt and embarrassment to leave in Jesus' Name.

Spiritually I bulldozed my way to get to the root of his helplessness. Beloved, when ministering deliverance you must get to the root of a person's issue. What good would it do them if you only take the leaves off of their heartache? You must be ready with your spiritual shovel and any other spiritual tools when ministering deliverance. Sometimes the roots of bondage in people's lives will take a few sessions to get to and pull up and sometimes it will be a very easy task. The Lord used me prophetically as well. I was instructed by the Holy Spirit to tear down and remove every negative word that was poured into his ear and to replace it with life. The more I called out the spirits of suicide, rage, murder, wrath, hate, and unclean spirits the more the demons were manifesting over the phone. Demonic spirits started to speak yelling to hang up so he doesn't have to hear my voice any more. I commanded those whispering and confusion spirits to flee and I also ordered them to shut their mouths.

When ministering deliverance you must be in control at all times. Spirits will try to intimidate you. While you are working you too are under attack. They will come to release doubt, fear, and feelings of inadequacies in you while you are working to get them out of the person free. Be mindful of this, but don't let it distract you. If the enemy can sniff out you are fearful, scared, or ill; equipped he will pounce on you as well. His goal is to get you so frustrated that you leave the person who is in need of freedom. I spent at least two and one-half hours on the phone with Brother Living. He was screaming, crying, sobbing, blowing his nose, which are all signs of deliverance. The Holy Spirit spoke to cast out unclean spirits. So, I proceeded to call out lust, perversion, and masturbation, lust of the eyes and in the flesh, sexual gluttony, and hidden sexual partners. Brother Living started to cough and I could tell those spirits were being pushed out, but kept trying to jump back down inside of him. I told Brother Living to lay hands on his throat; I started in like a battering ram with the names of the spirits the Holy Spirit was showing me. The more he showed me, I spoke it boldly and Brother Living kept throwing up more and more. I informed Brother Living of what was taking place, so fear would not set in again with him.

After this, I asked if he still wanted live. He replied, YES I DO! He said he never really wanted to die he just wanted help and to know God cares. I prophesied that it was going to get just a little hotter with the niece situation, but to hold on God was going to wipe it all away. I spoke that his family will heal; they will all be better as a result of it all. I prayed a prayer of protection and healing for his family. He thanked me and just kept saying how amazing God really is. He said he could not believe that God chose to answer his prayers and so swiftly. He was able to breathe and was now filled with hope for his situation. I then wanted to know what year he came out of high school because I did not think it was the same year that I had graduated. He told me the year and I said I was only in ninth grade that year. Now, I am looking at the phone puzzled. I asked what high school he attended; he gave me the name of a school that I never attended I said, "I thought we went to high school together." He said he thought he had heard me speak at another church. Neither was the case...in fact, we did not know each other at all until this particular day.

Look at God for his amazing alignment. He is so kind to always make a way of escape for us in our time of need. We both had a great laugh. He and his family came out to our Bible study. A couple of weeks later his wife called to let me know he was arrested for the situation involving her niece. Brother Living's wife and kids were in their car crying outside of the police station where he was being held. I told her it's not what it seemed. I spoke that the Lord needed him in the holding cell just for a couple of days. I told her there is a young male that needed to hear of God's saving and healing power. I told her he is on assignment in the holding cell. I said he will be out shortly with a great testimony and that all charges will be dropped against him.

Eight days later everything came to pass exactly the way the Lord had me to prophesy it. When you are operating in your anointing, you will not only operate in faith and boldness. There will be a peace in you to securely stand firm on what the Holy Spirit is sharing with you in hopes of settling another's spirit. Brother Living got home and gave my husband and me a call. He rejoiced in what the Lord did on his behalf. He was ecstatic and surprised how the

Lord used him in such a great way in the midst of his own hardships. He said he had to encourage another brother to live the same way the Lord used me for him. We were very happy this family seemed to be on the right road again. Sadly, Brother and Sister Living got a divorce. He kept the kids. She was caught in another relationship and pregnant by that man. Even though Brother Living's charges were dropped, Sister Living's family convinced her that he still did do those things. Sister Living believed her family and ended up leaving her husband and kids. In warfare, beloved there will be some casualties and loses. This particular time Brother Living lost his wife due to adultery.

## CASE STUDY: SIS. CAMILLE, PORTRAIT OF A BREAKTHROUGH IN HER SPIRIT

Sometimes deliverance for someone can come in the form of helping to soothe or ease their mindset. Comforting words can often times be the right medicine for people who need healing. We don't always have to lay hands on someone in order for them to get a breakthrough. I had a dream about a serious situation in a family member's life. In the dream, I saw my favorite uncle riding a bike holding his right side like he was in pain in our downtown city. When he approached me I saw he was crying and looking very confused. I asked what was wrong. He said that his girlfriend was in the hospital and he didn't know what he was going to do about it. He said she was very sick. He said, "Julie you must go to her and see about her... you must see what the doctors are saying."

Right after he spoke I was instantly in the hospital sitting right next to his girlfriend while she was receiving chemotherapy treatments. She kept telling me my uncle did not want to accept that she had cancer in her stomach. She said they just found out; it started in her stomach, but has now spread throughout her entire body. She asked me to get my uncle to understand what she was going through. She started to tell me how she looked forward to my visits because her family did not come to the hospital and how all of my encouraging words have been a blessing to her. Also in the dream she started to talk to me about God, how does his forgiveness work? Is it too late to repent? She even asked me about heaven and if I thought God would accept her in. I answered all of her questions and she was fully pleased with my answers. I told her how she needs to spend more time with Him now. I explained how important it is to forgive and love. I let her know how she was the apple of God's eye and He loves her a great deal. This made here smile in my dream. She then went to sleep. My uncle never made it in time to say goodbye. Then I woke up. It was about 7am.

I went about my day as normal. Later that afternoon, I had some church work to get done. My family and I were headed to our vehicle from our church on our way home. Before we could get into the car my favorite uncle and his girlfriend came driving down the street. They saw us and abruptly double parked. They rushed over to us and said they were looking all over for me. This was the time before cell phones. When Sister Camille got out of the car I saw her whole stomach radiating with bright primary colors. I tried not to stare at her. Then I asked myself was my dream was coming to pass. Instantly, I heard in my spirit not to lay hands on her; it is final. So, I figured my dream is now going to play out live and in color right in front of me. I asked the Lord to brace me and to give me the strength to hold in hold in all that I had seen prior in my dream.

He did just that too. Sister Camille started to tell us how she just found out that she has cancer. I asked cancer of the what? She replied in her stomach. Truth moment: my knees buckled a little. I also had not told my husband about dream. I only had time to write it down in my journal. I asked what stage was the cancer in she replied she didn't know. She said that she has an upcoming appointment to find out. She asked me to go with her to the appointment. I agreed. Meanwhile, my uncle was off to the side of our conversation telling my husband that it is not Cancer. Yes, clearly he was in denial about Sister Camille's medical condition. The appointment arrived and I went for support. She in fact had Stage 4 cancer, which started in her stomach and has now spread throughout her body. She was very sad. I did my best to encourage her. Now, I realized that my dream was actually coming to pass. I stayed by her side answering all of the same questions and concerns she had in my dream. Yes, her family would not come visit her. I did my best to comfort her with my words. Every day she thanked me for being there. She also said she had repented to the Lord and had found peace in Him. I never told her about my dream. However, my obedience and desire to see her again caused for her to come out of different bondages before she passed away. I asked God why I could not lay hands on her when I saw her in the natural. He told me that he loved me too much not to answer my prayers. He said He needed me in the position to comfort and restore someone that was supposed to go back to heaven with Him. He knew I would have pulled on him to keep her here with us for as long as possible. He assured me that I will see her again. Sister Camille passed away exactly one year to the day of my dream. Remember my favorite uncle was holding his side and never came back to see her? He died a year later to the day from Stomach cancer, too. This was a very challenging assignment. To know what was going to happen and not be able to speak on it was not easy. God's people need deliverance. They need to be rescued from bondage and danger. Some of which is due to their own mistakes, rebellion, and compromise. No deliverance situation is the same. But the end result should be... that the person is FREE!

# CHAPTER SIX

# WHAT'S IN A NAME? - GLOSSARY OF DEMONIC NAMES AND MEANINGS

Your name in the natural is very important to the proper function of your daily life. Identity: The collective aspect of the set of characteristics by which a thing is definitively recognizable or known (i.e., a name). Proper identification helps others to accurately know it is you and not someone fraudulently posing to obtain what rightfully belongs to you. Your name, age, social security number, and your address et cetera are all a part of your identity. When used properly you can be easily recognizable to who is in control of protecting your property and its distribution safely. For instance, after filling out all the initial paperwork in order to open a bank account, your next for a withdrawal is very easy due to your debit card having all of your identification information on it. In order to unlock your account to release your funds you must simply confirm your identity by entering your personal identification number (PIN) number.

Question: Now, if you do not have your debit card when you go to the bank how can you access the funds that are rightfully yours? Answer: through proper identification. In order to obtain the correct account without breaking confidentiality laws, the teller would ask you a series of questions. Sure they can get into all of the customer accounts. However, it would not do you any good until you give them the specific information that will pull up and unlock your personal account to give you exactly what you are asking.

When it's time for deliverance specific names are encouraged in order to assure the freedom of some individuals. Beloved, under the true anointing the enemy will try to hide from the deliverance worker in hopes of not having to leave the person's life. Can a person go through deliverance without specific demonic names being called out? Absolutely! But just think of how more a person could be free if the worker had more specific knowledge as to what spirits were in control. When you don't know a demon by name you can always call it out by the way it functions.

For example, I see a person who is in a reoccurring situation of no finances. If the person desires to be free from that and was ready to receive what the Lord had to say to them regarding the tormenting financial spirits it could be broken off of them. Even if I don't know the entire back side of the story, I would pray something like this:

*Father in the name of Jesus, I thank you for this individual. I thank you that no matter what picture the enemy has tried to paint for them they had enough strength to overcome his plans. Father in the name of Jesus, I break the spirits in their finances that are designed to keep their bank accounts in the negative, spirits that want them to always be the borrower instead of the lender, spirits that will keep them always wanting and needing and never being able to be full or content. In Jesus' name, I ask you Father to release a spirit of discipline in their lives for all that you have placed in their hands. In*

*Jesus' name, I declare that this individual will no longer depend on the world's system for provision, but will run to you the Author and Finisher of their faith for all things. In Jesus' name I pray. Amen!*

I do not know the reason why this person's bank account is always in the negative. However, that does not discourage me from praying effectively through the Holy Spirit on their behalf. Always be spirit led in prayer. Be very sensitive to the guidance of the Holy Spirit for He is the one that will always direct us unto truth and righteousness. So, remember, even if you don't know the specific name of a spirit in operation you can still remove it by calling out the way it functions and operates in a person's life.

Now, there are times where we must up our level of warfare knowledge when ministering deliverance. The Bible says that there are some spirits that will come out only through fasting and prayer (Matthew 17:21; Mark 9:29). Please beloved, do not into the strongman's house trying to bind him and the tables get turned and you're the one in need of saving all because you went in ill-equipped. The enemy can tell when you are unlearned and fearful. He knows when you don't have faith or even trust in the one you are calling on even while you're trying to go through a search and rescue mission for the Lord in the spirit.

**Okay, let's review, even if you don't know the official name of a demonic spirit you can still call it out by the way that it is functioning. However the more specific you can get the better the chances of freedom are for the individual receiving deliverance.**

Demons operate in groups. When someone is in need of deliverance it's never just one demonic spirit in operation, no matter what those spirits are saying back to you. Demons are very cunning and will do their best to play games with you. Never believe what they are trying to feed you. Discernment is key in all things of God. You must know what you are up against and if you are out of your league. If you don't know what you are trying to cast out of a person, the demonic spirits will know this and could possibly use this information to take advantage of you. The enemy does not play fair. He comes to steal, kill, and destroy... you. The worst state is the destroying. The enemy desires to annihilate you, never to see you rise again.

Take a lesson from the seven sons of Sceva in the book of Acts 19:11They thought casting out demons was cool and wanted to imitate Apostle Paul's anointing. Listen, do you know that your gifts and callings are without repentance (Romans 11:29)? Everyone is unique in what they can do in the kingdom of God. At times they can make it look so easy that anyone can do what they do. However, I promise you that it is a grace from the Lord upon that individual's life to minister the way that they do. Never try to imitate or duplicate what another person is doing, in the physical or in the spiritual. Embrace your uniqueness. You are a peculiar person divinely sent by God and guess what? You need to be okay with that.

The seven sons of Sceva saw that Apostle Paul's anointing was able to be transferred to handkerchiefs and aprons. People who received these items and who were sick in the body could be healed, diseases were removed, and demonic spirits were cast out. They, too, wanted to duplicate what was taking place. The Bible doesn't say why. However, nothing can ever prosper through a wrong motive or a dirty heart. The Lord will not bless your intentions in a matter, if pride is at the center of it all. What is the real reason you want God to use you prophetically, in deliverance, to preach and teach his word, or in going after the lost? If your rationale for wanted to be used by God is not coming from a place of compassion and caring, then it will fail. The word says that pride goes before a fall (Proverbs 16:18). Beloved, check your motives for wanting the Lord to use you. Is it because you believe you deserve to be used? Or you can be used better or greater than another individual? Or do you believe that what you can do or what you have to say is so phenomenal that it is enough to blow someone's mind or it is enough to deliver a massive amount of people? Beloved, this type of thinking and others like it is called pride. Do not allow the lust of your flesh to control you. Crucify your flesh daily. Do you not know that it only takes a little leaven to leaven the entire lump? (Galatians 5:9). In the Old Testament, leaven represented sin. Do not give sin permission to dictate your movements in God. Do not be so anxious to be used by God that you end up farther away from Him instead of being used by Him. Be reassured that your gifts really will make room for you and it really will bring you before great men (Proverbs 18:16).

When ministering deliverance and calling out what you are discerning is in control of a person, know that spirits operate in groups. I am listing some names of the strongman and the other possible spirits that would also be in operation. This listing is in no way the end all to be all listing. Please be led by the Spirit of God when ministering prophetically and through deliverance. This is what has helped me up until now. I use this list as the framework, but understand the Lord could shift what you are speaking on immediately.

I have learned that binding the strongman FIRST will allow for the others in operation to come out a little more easily. If the Holy Spirit gives you a different direction then by all means use it:

**Spirits of Rejection**
Low self esteem
Loneliness
Self-rejection
Self-hatred
Self-pity
Fear of rejection

**Spirits of Bitterness**
resentment
hatred
the inability to forgive
violence
murder
temper
anger

**Spirits of Rebellion**
stubbornness
disobedience
anti-submissiveness

**Spirits attacking the mind:**
bi- polar
schizophrenia
manic depression

**Spirits of Sexual Impurity**
lust
masturbation
homosexuality
lesbianism
adultery
fornication

**Spirits of Nervousness**
tension headaches
restlessness
insomnia

**Spirits of Depression**
despair
discouragement
suicide
hopelessness

**Spirits of Accusation**
judging
criticism
fault finding

**Spirits of Jealousy**
envy
suspicion
selfishness
distrust

When praying for someone in need of deliverance in the demonic groups referenced above, start by calling out the head name in the group and then start to rebuke the other spirits in the same group. When administering deliverance, you will pray, then prophesy, and cast out demonic spirits. This three-fold cord is not easily broken especially by the enemy (Ecclesiastes 4:12). While you are coming against these spirits, the Holy Spirit will give you discernment as to which way to go next.

Know this beloved, deliverance is a process. The individual did not get like that overnight so don't think you will cast out every demonic spirit overnight. Depending on the level of oppression may not be willing to get entirely free right away. Through the process some things will be revealed that the individual may have had locked up in them in hopes of never releasing and they are still not ready to release it all just yet. Do not try to be a deliverance one hit wonder use discernment, patience, caring, and kindness with the length of a deliverance session as well as its intensity. Demons will not cross a person's will if the person is not ready to be free in a certain area. They have just given legal rights to the spirits in operation to stay. In other words, you cannot go get what does not want to come out even though you know it is present. Pray that the Lord will protect the individual; so that if He so chooses to send you back to them that you will be ready to be used.

Warfare is needed in order to go after the ones in need of saving. We should never be the ones beating up, manipulating, or even belittling the individuals we have been charged in rescuing. The Bible says with loving kindness have I drawn thee (Jeremiah 31:3). **Question:** What is drawing individuals who are in need of saving to you? **Answer:** The anointing of God upon your life; the anointing that has the power to break yokes. Once you are successfully used by the Lord, remember to point people to Him, not you. Say this: *Lord harden my heart to the praises of man!* The Lord can use you in such a way that flattery will now be your reward, thusly tainting your heart. We cannot do anything without our Father. We are just His vehicles that He chooses to use during His search and rescue missions.

# CHAPTER SEVEN

FIRE IS NEEDFUL FOR OUR GROWTH - PRAYER CHANGES EVERYTHING

Beloved the word of God says, "...The effectual and fervent prayers of the righteous avails much" (James 5:16). Our Father in heaven loves for our prayers to be hot, sincere, bold, and full of trust. When you are in need of help and possibly saving, you most assuredly do not have time for pity pat types of prayers. When your life or that of your love ones is on the line you need to connect in the spirit to the one and only true, living savior our Lord Jesus Christ. You need immediate access to Him and His power to heal your situation. This is why the Bible tells us that we can come boldly to the throne of grace (Hebrews 4:16)

Come into agreement with these prayers with the mindset that God hears your prayers always. When speaking these prayers your heart must not be filled with doubt. Know that the Lord is waiting to hear from you. Trust that He hears you loud and clear the first time as long as you have a genuine heart for change to take place.

## WELCOME HOME PRAYER!

(A prayer asking for forgiveness and dedication back to the Lord)

Father in the name of your precious son Jesus the Christ, I first ask you for forgiveness. Forgive me for not believing in you. Forgive me for not following you a long time ago. Forgive me for turning my back on you when all you wanted to do was to love me. I know I have not done everything right in your or even my own eyesight. I thank you for loving me in spite of myself. I thank you for never giving up on me. I thank you for always believing in me to finally make the right decision to take up my cross and to follow you. Thank you for this brand new day! Thank you for being my joy, my peace, and my new found calmness. I thank you for always making ways out of no way and always providing for me even when I didn't deserve it. Today, Father I am ready to come home. This pig sty was never designed to be my dwelling place. The stench in the place that I am in is far to foul to bear. Father, I thank you for welcoming me back into your loving arms of safety. I no longer want to do things my way, but your way. I no longer desire my own will to be done, but yours instead. Father, please renew a right spirit within me. I want to please you in all my ways. I desire to be the head and not the tail like your word declares (Deuteronomy 28:13, 44). You said in your word that all of those who run to you will be protected from all harm and evil I desire that also (Proverbs 18:10). I'm grateful to be called one of your children today. I ask that you please continue to speak to me so I can understand your thoughts and plans for me (Jeremiah 29:11). I ask that you direct me to one of your houses of worship in order for me to grow more in the things that matter most to you. I love you and praise you! In Jesus' name, Amen!

# PRAYER AGAINST LOW SELF-ESTEEM AND SELF-HATRED

Father God, I'm turning to you the Author and Finisher of my faith (Hebrews 12:2). Lord, I trust that you know all and truly see all that concerns me and my life. Father, I really desire to smash and demolish every untrue record about myself, my history, and even what the enemy wants me to consider as being my impending future. I no longer will come into agreement with the unhealthy, ungodly images of myself that the enemy is holding up in front of me. Every vision of being less than, substandard, feelings of inadequacy, and even self-hatred for my mind, body, and spirit must dry up and die in Jesus' name! God, I choose to speak life to myself. I remember your word declares that you have made me (Psalm 100:3). I will declare how fearfully and wonderfully I am made (Psalm 139:14). At all times, I will declare how I am the apple of your eye (Zechariah 2:8) and your eye sight is always perfect. Lord, I fall out of agreement with what the world declares to be beautiful; I happily align myself with you and your word for my life. I thank you Father for allowing my views of myself, which were poor and lowly to finally arise from the ashes. I thank you for not giving up on me the way I had given up on myself. I am grateful for another opportunity to make you proud and to prove to all who will listen that I don't serve an abusive God, but a loving Father in heaven. Finally, I am free from this bondage and can honestly tell you thank you. Thank you for loving me, when I could not find the strength to love myself. Daddy, you truly are ALL I NEED! In Jesus' name, I pray. Amen!

# PRAYER FOR YOUR FINANCES

Dear Father which art in heaven, I trust you with everything I have and with everything that is soon to come. I break every untrue negative financial report. I speak that what and whom I currently owe will be settled immediately and sufficiently in Jesus' name. I speak that any and all debt will become a thing of the past. Father, you told me through your word in Romans 13:8, not to owe any man anything but love, which that is my sincere desire. According to your word in Proverbs 22:1 "A good name is rather to be chosen than great riches, and loving favour rather than silver and gold." Father, I desire a good name in repaying those I owe including paying what I owe to you in my tithes and offering. According to Psalm 37:25, You "...have never seen the righteous forsaken or his seed begging for bread." So, Lord, I thank you for always providing for me when I could not see any way out. Father, I break the curse of the cankerworm and locust from devouring all of finances before I have a chance to do good with it. I will no longer rob Peter to pay Paul. I will ensure restoration in the area of financial order. I will place you and your word first in my finances. I will make sure I give you a tenth of all of my increase. Father, I break and demolish the generational curse of welfare dependency, depending on others finances to keep me satisfied, the lack of respect for working hard, or for those that do. Father, I yield all of my finances over to you for proper decision making and management of my funds. I believe you are able to keep me from falling into financial ruin. I thank you that my finances and financial security is not in the hands of man, but safely in yours. I will no longer come into agreement with the spirit of the beggar, vagabond, or the wonderer. I will no longer entertain spirits of being financially immature and naïve. I will also fall out of covenant with the spirit of thievery, being a scam artist, and operating in deception. I thank you for being out of prison financially. I declare today is the first day toward creating and building legacy wealth for myself and generations to come. Father, I declare today that I will rest in the security of knowing that you desire the lines of my family and I to be healthy. According to Psalm 16:6 you desire to bring us into a beautiful inheritance and I receive it. In Jesus' saving name, Amen!

## PRAYER FOR YOUR CHILDREN

Father, in the name of Jesus Christ, I dedicate my children to you (Call each of your children by name). Lord God, I thank you for choosing me to be their parent. I repent of all neglect, disrespect, and trauma I may have caused my children. I ask for your total forgiveness in Jesus' name. I humbly ask for better parenting skills. Teach me how to parent and love just the way that you do. I no longer want to raise my children from what I only know or have seen. God, your word declares our children are gifts from you (Psalm 127:3). I desire to have complete appreciation for the gifts you have placed in my live. Your word tells me to train my children in the way they are to go so when they are old they will not depart from you (Proverbs 22:6). This, too, is my desire. Father, anything that was deposited into their spirits knowingly or unknowingly that will keep them from you when they are older I break its power right now in Jesus' Name. I declare that my children will be respectful and productive citizens. They will be atmospheric changers for the good. They will be the lender and not the borrowers (Deuteronomy 28:44), they will be great stewards over whatever you place into their hands. Father, I declare that they will love you continuously for the rest of their lives. I speak that they will fully understand and appreciate you as a youth and as adults they will not choose another way that seems right to them but the end thereof is death (Proverbs 14:12). Father, I thank you for trusting me with their spiritual, financial, emotional, and physical lives. Father, I thank you that after I repented for not living up to your standards as a parent that you are giving me another opportunity to make it right. Thank you for not giving up on me to parent and to love my children. I will not fail this most important assignment. In Jesus' name. Amen!

## PRAYER FOR YOUR SPOUSE

Father, I thank you for my help mate. I thank you for the love connection between us. I am grateful to you that we are still together. Everything may not be what we desire, but we still have you and each other. Father, I ask that you renew the spark of excitement for one another again. I ask in Jesus' name that the enemy, who loves division in families, not win in my marriage. I speak life into every dead area of my marriage. I ask for forgiveness for abusing, neglecting, manipulating, and controlling through being proud towards my spouse. I am now willing to forgive the same from my spouse for harsh and brash treatment. I speak we will honor our marriage commitments made before you on our wedding day. Thank you for loving our union even when we could not see the value in it. Because of that love I/we are now rededicating our marriage and all of its inner workings to your leading. In Jesus' precious name, Amen!

# CLOSING THOUGHTS

Singing....
Rejoice in the Lord always
And again I say, again I say
Rejoice in the Lord always
And again, I say again I say
REJOICE!

Beloved, I pray that you laughed, cried, received deliverance, and now are feeling empowered to be about your Father's business. This book was another labor of love. I pray that you heard my heart through these written words. I believe that from this point on you will no longer walk in condemnation of your past; but that your mind is now renewed, restored, and transformed. This is just the beginning for you. Hold your head up, do not give up, nor give in! Know that the race is not given to the swift...but to those who endure to the end (Ecclesiastes 9:11; Matthew 24:13). My sincere prayer that you will stay true to you! Never give anyone permission especially, not the enemy to dictate who you are or are destined to become. Did you know beloved that your success is medicine for all of those who are dying from lack of it? Our Father in heaven has built you to last. So compromising in the things of God or just in your own personal life is no longer an option. Know that it is not what others think of you, but only what you do for Christ that matters and that will last. Lastly, never allow the peace that you are now walking in to be disturbed by another's instability. I really want to encourage you to change the world while refusing to let it change you! Beloved, today, submit yourself to the Lord and resist the devil and I promise you he will flee...from you!

-Apostle J

www.ingramcontent.com/pod-product-compliance
Lightning Source LLC
Chambersburg PA
CBHW071631040426
42452CB00009B/1574